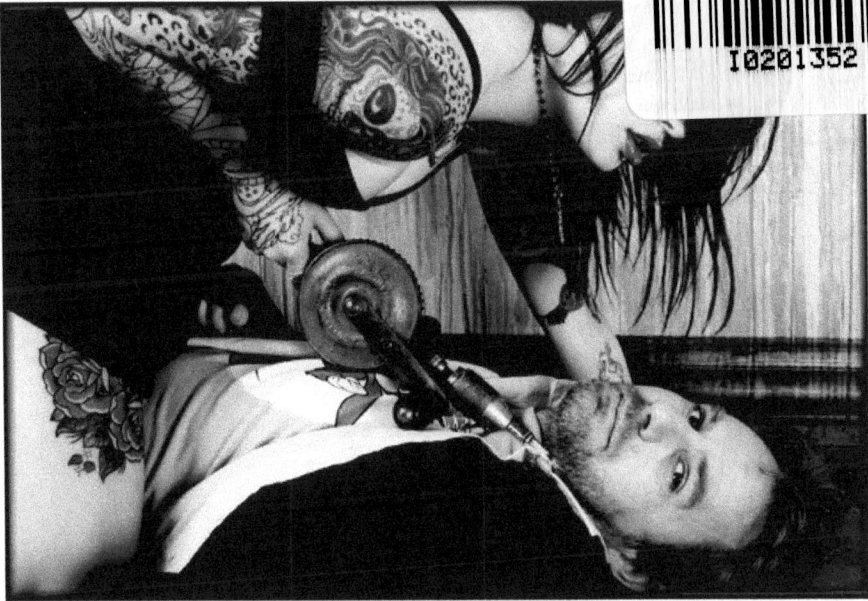

A flawed romantic with a predilection it seems for self destruction, Sean King's words have a hint of Bukowski, more than a tipple of Algren, maybe even a little Crews but unlike so many pretenders to the throne, King isn't trying to be anyone but himself. And though he tries to come across as hardboiled, as tough and mean, a singular man who needs no one but himself, his vulnerability still shines through, the belief that it can get better, that things can improve, this belief hovers underneath the words, sometimes barely heard, barely seen but it is there none the less. You just have to know where to look.

Sean King takes the essence of human existence, chops it up finely, divides it smoothly into lines with a maxed out credit card and leaves it on a cracked glass table for you to snort up with a rolled twenty dollar bill. Of course it ain't pure, it never is. No, this has been cut with alcoholism, despair, greed, fear, jealousy, love and lust – but King knows that stuff won't kill you since you've got plenty of it floating around in your system already. We're all flawed but not that many of us will admit it. Sean has and now it's your turn. Take that twenty, roll it up, take a deep breath and get ready for the rush.

Kami

Like the Dog I Am
Sean King
re-published by seankingonline.com

Copyright © Sean King 2012

PO BOX 710
Brighton
South Australia
Australia 5048
www.seankingonline.com

First Published 2012

Cover Design: Sean King
Cover Photograph Main: Kelly Jade King
Photographs back cover and inside: Kelly Jade King
Typeset by seankingonline.com
ISBN 978-0-9872927-8-0

# LIKE THE DOG I AM

# BY

# SEAN KING

*For my red headed pixie who understands me more
than I understand myself sometimes...*

# MAN OF THE WORLD

Spank fuck
Man of the world
From a couch bathed in arrogance

Go fuck yourself

And fuck the world that resides
Inside a head
Your head
Not sure of what it should be

Go fuck yourself

And the attitude
That rides upon your
Lazy shoulders
Your excuses
Your bad taste

Your inability to understand the reality the rest of us fight every day

Mummy can't help forever

Mummy can only change so many nappies

Mummy can't hold out much more

Man of the world
With little more than the walls around you
The cotton wool that wraps you tightly
And a plethora of tired excuses

Go fuck yourself

And fuck your lack of reality
Your lack of thought
Your lack of life

Spank fuck
Man of the world
Go fuck yourself

And don't ever knock on my door again

For help

For advice

For a shoulder

For when that inevitable time arrives
I will laugh you from this world
And mock your bad decisions
And take solace in the fact
That once
Once
I reached a helping hand your way
And like the rabid animal you pretend not to be

You tore it from my arm in mislead arrogance...


## THE WOMAN NOBODY KNEW

She was always there
In the back of my mind

The woman nobody knew

A cold night
After few, but all so warm
She never said why
She never said what it was that turned her sour that made her dislike

I'm sure it was my writing, that she didn't understand the words that came from my pen

It was through
Misinterpretation

Misinformation
Mis...s

I wrote about her, about paintings that passed me by every day
Paintings of dancers
Paintings of beauty
About long blacks
And
Intellectual tennis
About stars not moving
But ground instead

And I didn't write about her as well

That woman nobody knew

The Middle East is coming
And going
Like the slight catch of an autumn breeze
Or the bullet shot from a gun in a bricked alleyway
And even these few words
About the woman nobody knew...


## *THE RIDE*

I rode a park bench to hell one day
alongside blue skies to nowhere
dreaming endlessness
to breezes content to fleet past with no more than a whisper
or a slight flick of tangled hair
retribution in its nothingness
a hell made pretty
by its ill-fitted clash with my mood
words are no longer my friend
and time
a greater enemy than ever before
the raw and young lust of achievement
merely a sniff of the
pollution
within which we all now sit...

## SHE

her shoulders were bare in the loose top
I told her she had a body like death and then we went back to her place
and fucked
she never said much
but when she did
it was in a monotonous life-draining drawl

then her husband came home
and I
out the back door
clothes bunched in arms
to jump neighbors fences
and catch testicles
on the rusty nails of my life

## WEDNESDAYS LIKE HEMINGWAY AND JEWS AND FREEDOM

she came around on a wednesday. it was after hearing that i had
destroyed my life and severed my love. again no less. she bought wine
with her. i don't drink wine. i can't drink wine.

"here, i bought wine."

i poured us a couple of glasses as she settled in for an attempt at the
long haul. alcohol, it seemed, was where i was being drawn again. an
inability at peace and quiet the only draw card to fuel further hatred at
what i had become. i guzzled. the taste was like acid and acid was just
what the order of the moment turned out to be.

"so," she said, "i was reading your book again today." "yeah. my book.
my blatant attempt at creating some type of self-justification for the
fucked-up-ness of my wandering mind." "your work is good. Sometimes
too good." "my work is my honesty and my honesty is my downfall. you
of all people should understand that." "honesty hurts people. i know.
you've told me that before." "I've told you many things before but it's
never made a difference. to life. to us. to the world around us. words,
that's all they ever were. it's all my life ever has been."

drinking another glass amidst a silence that emanated undertones of her sexuality and my discontent, proved only to scare me into the reality that alcohol could be my downfall like it came so close to being so many years ago. with that i grabbed the bottle and re-filled our glasses. she was wearing a dress. it was a short dress and her thighs seemed large. enticing. like crystal clear water on a steaming day, or a loaded gun when it all becomes far too much. like it is now.

"you know i've always loved you. wanted you." she moves those thighs when she speaks and i see a glimpse, though ever so slight, of blue panties. it stirs my rampant groin. "so you've said. look babe, i don't know what to say to that. i want to fuck you. i want to fuck you right now, right here. and then i want you to go away. i don't need this. christ. i can't even get it together enough to eat. all i do is sit here in this dark room, this dark world and this dark mind and drink bitter coffee after bitter coffee and smoke cigarette after cigarette writing words in a pad that will never see the light of day. i'm destroying myself from the inside out and it's all i can do."

she puts her glass down and opens those thighs of steel. i get a longer look at those panties and the shape of that wet pussy, that animal instigator. i get a glimpse at my downfall. at every ones downfall. i get a glimpse at my immediate future and i wonder, for just a short, short moment in time, whether women were put on this earth to destroy the male population in an attempt to maintain a needed male/female balance.

glass down and legs again closed she moves from her chair to work on my zipper while i sip at the red and create great fantasies about a world with no rules where dogs of war no longer dictate the futures of masses they have never met let alone cared for in any way. she sucks hard and she sucks well though not as well as the last, or the one before that. but close. is this what it all comes down to? the animalistic desire to sow your seeds through fornication? we are the animals. just like the cats and lions and birds and snakes and elephants and insects. our only difference is the ability to hate so much between the moments of desire to nurture and carry on the species.

and with the moment she stands and removes her dress. that dress, the cover that's worn through shyness and prudence and more.

that dress which now lies humped at feet still encased in bright red heels. her breasts are quaint with no real shape yet already the sign of age drags them toward the ground. antiquities in the making. gravity. the force that works against us all. and thumbs locked in the bands of those revealing and blue panties drag downward while that very gravity contradicts the outcome and makes the whole show an awkward attempt at sexy.

"fuck  me," she says.

i empty the last of the wine from the bottle, drop it to the ground, assess the sixties bush and wonder whether i now sit in a time warp. a non-reality. free love that is never really free. freedom that is just a covert word for restriction put in place to stop the writers writing the rapists raping and the germans from ever having to admit their stupidities.

i drape her over my chair.

i fuck her hard.

she moans and i wonder about those moans. are they real or just the need of an expectation set by the very same society that dictates we live by a mythological list of commandments put in place as a means of excuse to get rich, to justify dictation. i opt for the latter with all disdain and drive harder and faster like it's a last ditched attempt to get across the finish line. of life. of life. the finish line of life. and i fuck her and she moans and i fuck her harder and she moans harder and harder and harder and it all means jack shit at the end of the day the year the world and life.

she orgasms and i don't because i just don't anymore. the pleasures derived from life are far and few between and this whore that now lies panting and sweating and semi-ejaculating over my life is no exception to the rule. i don't come because this outer shell is all that's left and i don't come because i don't exist anymore than a leper's fantasy for a long life full of love and sexuality. i don't come. i can't.

i push her out the door. throw those blue panties out after her. she looks hurt and frightened and confused and i don't care about that either. you got what you came for and now it's time to leave me alone. go. go. go gossip about your glory and your pride and tell the lies you so need to tell to make it seem different than what it really was. go. go live your life in your bubble while clinging desperately to your dreams. go. go. go. i have. i did. and i never came back. that is the reality of what awaits. nothing more and nothing less.

"but why?" she pleads in all her femininity. "because like hemingway and jews and freedom and truth...i am dead."


## THE WEATHER

a comment about the weather
was all it took
for ned
to snap into a rampage
his wife was gone
took his kid too
worse
took all the money
he jammed the knife home
straight through that fuck's chest
the crunch of bone
the squelch of organs as it made its way through
the spraying of blood
they found ned
there
on the ground
his neighbor
bloody... dead... and by his side
they found ned
there
just as dead
inside

## CYCLE

blinding light and instant classification as the all new stands before
you in an unchartered mystery of new sight and sound and touch
where exploration seeks gratification and gratification retribution.
then people then learning then restriction and rule like chains of
invisibility too tight to scramble free of if only realization has hit
so early and as lucky or unlucky you are as few and destined to
critique. more of the same dished under the banner of education
sent for the satisfaction of a zombie nation shadowed in black and
tarnished by the red of the ever noncompliant who stand against
the attempts of destruction of choice where willingness is sought.
wading through the blood from shackle to shackle then love of
women or men fraught with the same tarnished brush as all those
around over under and between where hearts are torn and trusts
lost and lives given over to the sadness and the shallowness and
the insecurity and the need to be as two one none to find yourself
again seeking the exact same hurt previously experienced though
never learned. your road your wheels of two of speed hoping for
that rabbit that cow that imperfection upon the service you now ride
and disappointed you are when these dares don't show themselves
to the light you thought you were running toward (or away from?)
perhaps. you turn again and delve so deep into the politics of life
the rules of love the journey toward loneliness where loneliness lies
to those around to heart to soul though nothing you say or do or
feel shall make the slightest of difference on the madness that we
all call ourselves. of word of thought of book of paper of unsatisfied
need to throw yourself from the edge to the wind that will carry you
forward or drop you from the sky to the rocks below awaiting like
the vultures that society are but you can't though you will if only you
could and you shall when the time seems right and the moon stills
before turning the blood red of all the fears you have been taught
to carry. of decay and in decay you sit you feel you don't feel and
can't feel through the numbness of the years while your nose itches
and stings from the tang of decayed death that sits around you that
taunts around you that screams to you that your time will come
though soon it is it will not rest it's purpose clear within your fear
and spite the desire to scream and shout and resist the inevitable
you understand your mortality accept your fate. blackness and
the new smell of the dirt that now and forever remains your final

salvation and protection and comfort and peace. the cycle...

## ONE PACK OF LIFESTYLES AND TWELVE BOXES OF NO-DOZ THANKS...

It happens every now and again, you turn around to find that you have suddenly and mysteriously become an "option" for the bedding of the opposite sex. From zero to 100 in three flat seconds, fasten your racing harness and prepare for the "cocktail[ish]" variety that suddenly awaits your tasting attentions.

From "not really my type" to "if I sleep with her am I ever going to be subject to arousal by any other woman again", you don your armor and march forth, head on with no look backward, determine to do it for all mankind. It's your responsibility, your primal urge and above all your testament to the animal that lies beneath the surface of all of us. Besides, you know that their interest will wane again at some point in the near future and you will find yourself pulling your hand from your pocket and vigorously forcing it to RSI status once again.

Sometimes successful and standing on the ridge of the battlefield, sword high in the air, at others not quite as good as you wanted to be, you draw knowledge from the subtle differences between each of your experiences and at times sigh, while others, you smile more than ever before.

You feel unstoppable. Hormones wild and juices running it's almost as if you have walked into your very own Lynx commercial as the one and only star. How long all this lasts is a mystery but for the briefest moment you smile to yourself when you open your glove box searching for sunglasses only to be greeted by a pack of Lifestyles and a box of No-Doz...

## SELF PORTRAIT

he lives next door
rides a motorcycle
has grown a beard
and is in love with a little red haired girl that looks like a pixie and
smells like the sweetest essence of coffee on a cold morning

he has a daughter that rides his heart as well as a rodeo queen at
the peak of her career
and he smokes cigarettes
and flies to exotic locations on sleepless nights
his hair's getting long
and, he sometimes reminds himself of hobos riding box cars in the
days of old
- no destination
some call him a loser
others a genius

but he doesn't care much for any of it
he just wants people to
go
fuck
themselves

and leave him be...


## DOG'S BUSINESS

He couldn't be around dogs. Or dog owners for that matter. The
problem wasn't the dogs (or owners) themselves, but more his
uncontrolled response to the owner's commands. You see, ever
since an early age, whenever someone told a dog to sit his own
mind would take control of his body and he too, would find himself
sitting. It really was all quite awkward.


## THE 8-6-3 TO SHITSVILLE

back
on the 8-6-3 to shitsville
all the regulars are here
the man and his boy who seem more like friends than a father
taking his son to school
the old woman's here too - she always gets on with coffee held in a
hand so shaky I wonder how much she actually gets to drink
the guy on the phone, the one with squinty and crossed eyes who
talks so loud we all know what he's doing tonight, tomorrow, next
week - he's divorced now but that's ok because he's met someone

willing to put up with him, willing to stick by him the way his wife
didn't after the accident "sure" I want to say to him show me a
woman that willing and I'll show you how well the world lives in
harmony and peace
there's the hot chick with legs longer than my life so far and straight
blonde hair who always seems to wear clothes that are so much
older than her years
I wonder why she does that and can't answer as much as I can't
answer the questions about my own life
I'm back
on the 8-6-3 to shitsville
where all the drivers can't drive and all the regulars  live lives
mundane like television on a Sunday
the 8-6-3
that takes us all to shitsville
to live our lives the only way we can...

...with debt in one pocket and society's finger up our arse


## *I NEVER SAID ENOUGH*

I never said enough
when her dad died
I should have
been  there
to hold her hand
to burden her tears
to take her anger
like I wanted to be

but I never said enough

I wasn't the man
I should have been
instead
cowering from my hurt
and love
cowering from myself

I let her down

at the worst time
of her young life
let her down
because I never said enough

and still
I can't...


## THE EMPTY BUS

I'm in a bus
It's raining outside
Just like it is on the inside
The bus is crowded
Though
In my mind
My heart
It is as empty
As I am
All I see
Is the vision of you
Walking the aisle toward me
And telling me
What I know
You want to say


## THE BLACK STALLION

one part of me stands so far to the left
the other
sits to the right
the balance
so far outweighed
guilt gallops past me on a black stallion
too fast to do anything, yet slow enough to tap me on a shoulder
which lays ignorant to the now
feelings for convenience
feelings because I feel I have to have them and on the other
side feelings I have no control or choice over

I know where I want to go
where I want to be
how I want to go there
I just don't understand how to get there
Isn't it true that it is the things that you can't understand
can't control
that can't be wrong?

He Won't Win...........


## *LAVENDER*

lavender
in a sea of khaki
an enemy
of both states
I keep seeing red from the corner of my eye
but it's not the red I want to see
the church grounds I have always feared so much
I can see in a different way today
a different light...


## *RASPBERRIES FROM THE BACKSEAT*

Minds
Two
But somehow the same
Naked
Two
But one
So close
So right
I wake
In the wake
And still
I feel like I am
Naked
Blowing raspberries from the backseat of her life

It's like being diabetic
And pounding away at the sugar
Her sugar
Knowing very well
That all that may result Is the death
That is expected
And again
I smile
I hope
I dream
While I
Sit here
Naked
Blowing raspberries from the backseat of her life


## BLOWING THE NIGHT

I found myself standing in a decrepit city toilet block, again, my pants around ankles swollen from my journey so far. A crack whore between my legs, I draw on my last cigarette and blow the blue stream of smoke at walls distended with years of blood, sweat and tears. Years of street violence and the realities of lives most choose to pretend don't exist. It's almost as if the walls absorb the smoke rather than reject its cancerous presence, like the decay of its life so far instills more fear than dying the hidden death.

Slurp. Slurp.

Smack.

The whore continues her practiced duties while I wonder what it's all come to. A woman, a thing, performing oral on strangers all in aid of another hit of substance that will drain her life from her very soul for the smallest of moments in time. She's already dead, just like the rest of this ugly god damn world. The only difference is that they don't know it. And here we both stand / kneel, two dead people, each contributing to the over-stressed pockets of the lords, to the lifestyles of the rich.

I snarl at the shadowed corners and notice that the only remaining light in the room is covered with what could only be the stench and darkness of the whole concept of degradation. I wonder just what atrocities this very light may have witnessed in this nighttime prison, this realm not known to those who believe the world they live in is so fucking perfect.

A siren begins its chant of authority far in the distance. It reminds me of the illegality of what I now receive from this toothless, used up whore of the night. Hah! The law. What law? The one that beats at the un-deserving? The very law that protects the real criminals in this shithole world while the rest of us are made to suffer? The thought disgusts me and I inwardly spit on the contradiction of the whole thing. I would really love to scream my dissatisfaction at the top of my lungs but the silence (other than the smack, smack, smack of the mouth on my shaft), is just proof of my oppressed self. Solid proof of the silence I have held so long despite never being so ignorant to it all.

This bitch just isn't going to get me off. I realize it so push her wrinkled face from my groin without any desire to be gentle. Slumped on the floor in an awkward pose she looks up at me with blank eyes and a questioning expression. I'm sure she sits there wondering in all her mess whether she's still going to receive the twenty she's been working at.

Despite my hate for everything on this foul night I just can't bring myself to leaving her unrewarded for her attempts regardless of how fruitless they have proven to be on this occasion. Yeah, even I sometimes have enough heart to realize that effort has to count for something.

Not bothering to zip up my pants I pull twenty from my pocket and drop it on the whore as I step past her useless and slumped skeleton. Once upon a time in what seems like a completely different life, I would have cared about what happened to this shadow of a woman, worried for her even. But tonight.

Tonight...

## A TEXT MESSAGE

well there's some blog material rolling off my hand like words from the tongue of a linguist affected by hate by love by desire and society but most of all by women. I think and I don't think which leads to thinking again and you should be here but at the same time you shouldn't because there is only so much desire to be taken before life gets in the way and walls mysteriously construct because they are the only way to protect heart soul and possibly sanity. I ask myself whether I should just walk and never look back for your sake and for that of the world because maybe just maybe they wouldn't be able to handle being treated the way you would or feeling the way you should but don't because you can't and I can't and fuck knows because fuck knows everything and everyone and then my daughter asked about you tonight because she can feel so much about me and what I am feeling and I'm going to stop because I really don't know what I'm saying and you might stop talking to me because you think I'm a freak and then I would hate me even more though I couldn't anyway and FUCK

## A LOVE STORY ABOUT LOVE BUT NOT LOVE

I WANTed to write a story about love and the LOSS of it and the heartache and the constant SLEEPLESS nights and the lack of desire to eat drink talk or even move and when I sat down to think about all of this I realized that I was at the very moment in exactly the same position the same MINDSET the same degree of SADNESS and feeling of hopelessness that I may just have felt had I have lost her again

maybe even worse

INSOMNIA bought on by a mind too geared up to create and write and think infected by a woman more BEAUTIFUL than ever before known to the single creates the darkest of hours when daylight is too much and the darkness of night not enough yet it all is enough if only she would press those buttons once again send that message with undertones of LOVE and implications of her own HEARTACHE and DESIRE and insomnia and delight for response and need to interact with me and only me and no one else except me the me that she is learning to know and liking more and still loving despite the ill fortunes of UNDERSTANDING my darker side and darker past

is inevitability a danger of the heart?

FACTITIOUS reasoning bought on by the non-consumptions of TRUTH wielded through the powers that be and are and will forever remain from birth through death like the cycle of a butterfly though unluckily not so quick she JUDGES and over thinks and worries about too much instead of moving forward with the wave creating the momentum required to catch and to ride and to enjoy the force by which their love has so MYSTERIOUSLY been forced upon them in matters of instant though withheld for too long and RECOGNISED only as a threat that needs to be kept in CAGE she finally realized the TRUTH her truth her very own DECEPTION of her SOUL and though not too late when does this become too late like missing the train for a second time when things may just be preventing the rush that could possibly be required as the FOUNDATIONS and bricks are so SUBCONSCIOUSLY forced into place and the wall finds itself being so rather than a figment of histories imagination

I digress

there was only ever one that TOUCHED so deeply so COMPLETELY who had the arms the heart the soul to truly move beyond that wall of discontent and FEAR and non-desire and yet now there is TWO and ONE has become two yet is still just one because one remains so long ago but not before the mortar was in place the divine creation of a hate and fear and disgust at the deceptions that are and always will be the world and the people in the world the children who are learning to be just like the adults who truly seek the MINDSET of selfishness and non-justice and external hate and lie like dogs all dogs and doomed to self-righteousness and self-infliction but never SELF disgust because to disgust oneself one must recognize first the implications of their very own demeanor

and so it is I am horrid

because horrid is what horrid does and too judging is the only judging and too much heart makes for too much pain yet harshness comes so easily when desperation seems to hover but never over embellish as one grasps at a dream of years in creation and fears losing that dream all over again yet not losing it at this moment in a too fast time seems all the more for pain while the moments together always remain cinematic and triumphant to both and deserved and real and natural and so full of comfort like lying in the sun as a cool breeze gently caresses and takes from the sting he knows how much of a gentle breeze she is for him and he hopes the same for her he reaches to her in his mind embarrassed and apologetic at his obvious pushiness and knows that even should she know she understand she smile that it may very well push her from him

make love to me forever

 if only once  I miss you I miss you

alone with them with her

OPPORTUNITIES with no want no desire no need no soul alone could be the greatest answer where silence is BLISS and SEX is the bitch on the corner of a darkened street though them are many and them are BEAUTIFUL and them are sexy no them is her and no beauty or SEXINESS would ever surpass what is her and always has been her to him he hopes she feels the same as she wanders the hallways of popular stride and over PASSIONATE offer amidst the world of her and those around hers creation a world apart a lifetime apart but closer than the warmth that touches ones skin and corners of dark whores  with no retribution and no feeling and no real desire or reality where sterility is the part and transaction is the order may very well be in compensation for loss yet he thinks not now and hopes not now and DESIRES not now

all he can do is click

and hope

and smile

at the moments they so dearly share in a love story made for the
eyes of the screen and the hearts of two


## MAYBE YOUR LAST

you grab your boots
your guitar
and your fear of tomato soup
and head out into the world
content with your knowledge
that what you've got
is all you have
what you have
is all you've got
and your next
kiss
smile
tear
cigarette
may be
your
last...


## LOOKING AT YOURSELF IN A NON-REFLECTIVE MIRROR

I know routine
better
than routine knows itself
I know
temporary heroes
like comic books
burnt
at the whim of boredom

I know passion
misconstrued as love
borders of mistrust
and misuse
and

abuse

I know life
at both ends of the razor
and darkness
and light
and the fright
of looking at yourself
in a
non-reflective
mirror


## LESS IN TIME THAN ANY COULD GUESS

the incessant jumping of the CD
in the background
pounds through my head without respite
am I the only one that notices?

or is it my imagination
laughingly
mocking me into false thought?
and ever more false
anticipation

of an end to the rhythms
that drive it's madness
my madness
and that of those around

I no longer care for sunshine
or rain
or wind
don't eat through want
or fly in over imagined non-reality
alongside those that may never
give up the dream

no

I live it
and I breathe it
and I nurture the love it brings
at smallest moments
moments
less in time than any could guess
or know

and all the while

she stands beside me
though unseen
and un-known
and
dead to all
but me
and whatever existences may live outside what we all could ever
know
I trip

and my beating heart
falls to the pavement
once again...


## CALLED POLITICS, CALLED RELIGION, CALLED SOCIETY

all these people
drinking
mixes made to help them forget
their lives
of working
not
for themselves
but for
the men

alcohol
the love of yesterday
lost
to better judgment

or not
like slowly splitting
the skin
of sunburnt wrists
with
razors
made from rust
or cancer
whichever you prefer

poets
hating mornings
hating days
hating nights
while moments are spent
wrapped in ideas made to mask
the sweetest of poisons
called
politics
called
religion
called
society

drink people

consume

and continue your slowly
deaths
when the light next
returns...


## RUNNING

He pulls into a gas station. A town. Somewhere, but he's not sure
where. He's not sure of anything. It's three a.m. and the gas pumps
are closed. He doesn't care because he is not here for that. He's
here because the driving became too much. Driving that kept
reminding him that he was running away. He's here because he

needs to hit something. Hard. Solid. He needs the distraction of physical pain to remove that which he is feeling so deep within. The ripping of his soul for a second time and, he knows, also the last. He's not a violent person, nor one that resorts to self-infliction, but he realizes that frustration could, at this point, be his most worst of enemies.

Like all things cinematically delivered to his tired mind, he sees the rest room for what it is - a blatant disrespect for any other than oneself. A mess of tangent odor and a dampness canvassed by broken tiles, door less cubicles and the shit of previous dignitaries who have happened by these very same restrooms. Disgrace doesn't concern him. It is a disgrace of his very own that he now flees from. He wonders. Should it have been any different?

He whispers her name to no one and it echoes around the walls, penetrates deep into the corners of the room before returning to him over, and over again. Much the same as it has within his dreams. The only difference the tear that now moves from the corner of his eye, dragged by gravity toward an existence alongside the slop of the room. A tear that just days before, was a smile of uncontrollable joy at what he always dreamed of having. He wishes he could follow that single tear but knows he can't. He still exists in other people's minds and they need him as much as he feels he needs her to be the complete man he should always have been.

The reflection that stares back through the cracks in the damaged mirror seems un-familiar to him. He's never known this man, this thing that stares back with discontent. The mocking in the eyes of this once familiar stranger remind him of his very own indifference to those that have had to suffer at his hand throughout this time. "Payback," he hears, "payback is the biggest bitch." Could those tired, red and now colorless eyes really be his? Could that voice which now speaks to him from deep within the grime of neglect be chanting those very same words he dreamt about?

The moments are black before he finds himself running from fear, running from that man, that thing in the mirror. His car. The road. His safety. Fleeing again but this time, not from her but him. A writer who cannot write and a poet who no longer holds the desire for words that once lived within. Another cigarette and painful reminders as he pulls the tiny shards of mirror from his hand, he cries now more than he has forever. It's good. The pain feels good and the wetness of his cheeks instantly chilled by the force of wind through his open window feels good. Could it really be that the hint of a smile crosses his quivering lips?

It's her again. Right there in his mind. She sits in her car in the middle of the street and awaits him. He approaches, leans in and her voice, a sound of water trickling along a winter stream, whispers to his ear, "I love you too." Outside lights from the tarnished windows highlighting the renaissance perfection that is herself in purity and smiles of contentment and joy that grace those very lips that gently portray the feelings she holds for him as she brings them to his own.

"I love you too." She had said it to him before, her desire to avoid him never hearing those sweet words should he walk away and never be seen again driving her to the truth within herself. He knows that should he be patient, should he hold himself for time, through time, that she would return to him again. Be it a year, or two, or even three, she would be back in his arms and ready to spend her life with him. Is he that selfish? Is he that hard that he could not wait that time again? Could he let her walk away a second time in the hope that she would return or would that, for him, be the ultimate self-punishment? To suffer again in secret at what has been and what could have been? He knows he can't. He knows how second he would feel. He knows how well he could hurt, how well she could hurt him by that very contempt.

Turning the car he now drives again, toward her now rather than the away that has so far been. Too fast, yet not fast enough, confusion takes the reigns. Stopping. Starting. Stopping again, the blood from his knuckles forming its crust around his soul. He leaps from the idling car and lands in the middle of the cold dark road, stares to the sky in search of answers to all that he has asked.

And as always, none seem to come...

## *DEAD CHILDREN ON DEAD STREETS*

Down the interstate in a
big red car
topping 150 like an accountant
shredding the evidence
past the pink flamingos that
don't exist
heads stuck in white
picket fences blurred by change
throwin' dimes at passers
by
the black the red the
yellow the white
screamin' ding dong the
witch is dead
and following phantoms
without any heads
up looks down while down
looks up
and I speed sideways
through rusty memories and
the bottom of too-soon-ending
alcohols

rushing

rushing

rushing

towards what?

vision has no end no goals
vision has no wisdom

another cigarette another
dead animal more excuses
with no reason to blink
excessive and obsessive are
a marriage in heaven for

the falling leaves the falling
stars the falling men and
women and children of a
backward rotating world

gone mad

unsticking the stuck like
popping the cork on a
dusty once forgotten
bottle of fine, fine
red

160

170

180

speed past the poor
at the end of a stick
swung by the blue

past the dead children
on the dead streets of
a city dead of love

no mind for no time
cause time moves as it
likes across the faces
of the people
shadows
fast and extreme

we all
swallow our suns
sometime ...

## BLACK COFFEE

I'm sitting here
right here
not there

and
I'm sitting here
drinking black coffee

I'm drinking it here
black
and
strong
and smokin' cigarettes
hard
and long

and you see

you see
I'm thinking about
the dream I had
cause I had a dream

I had a dream
that I fell off a building
and when I fell off that
building
and I was falling
I passed a banker

I passed a banker
and I said
man...

man what are you doing here
and the banker
the banker just looked at me
with big banker eyes

and he told me
that he was sick
that he was sick of no love
he told me
that he knows they
call him a wanker
that banker

wanker

and he was sick of it
and I said to him
I said
man
we've all been called a
wanker once in our life

and he just smiled
he just smiled
and fell
because he knew
he knew
that it was his time
that it was his end

and so I sip more
black coffee
and smoke more cigarettes
while the waitress
with no eyes
keeps my cup full
and tells me

she tells me
bout a man
down the road a bit
at a club called 49

she tells me
that he promised to

marry her
and give her a house
with a white picket fence
that goes from here
to there

from here all the way
to the moon and back

and I tell her

I say
babe
we've all broken promises
once in our lives

but she doesn't hear me

she just stares
that waitress with no eyes
because
you see

she has a dream

and sometimes

sometimes
a dream is all that
keeps us going


## WE NEVER SLEPT TOGETHER

she wants me to love her

we stand
overlooking the Savannah of both our pasts
do you think we can make it she asks

(the frogs will only return to the ponds if there is water)

we watch the world go by
puppets
in a marionette
they all walk the same lost in transition
soulless waves pushing them forward

waiting for a monsoon
for the feel of the rain
for the damp cheek
we stand

I smoke

I wonder

dark clouds brew
distant thunder touches the ear and slightly vibrates the nerve

we never slept together
we never woke
to sunlit mornings and bitter coffee with nothing to do but lay in the
warmth of the mist that would have been

yet still we stand overlooking the Savannah

and still

she wants me to love her

ants in a world of self-destruction

no-one ever looks up
why does no-one ever look up?

and I smoke I wonder

we never slept together
always apart in distance
always surrounded by those who like all others never look up

are we hidden up here
in a place they call heaven

a misinterpretation of the desire to carry on though nothing is left

I shudder
I smoke
I wonder

and she wants me to love her and we never slept together and up is too hard and frogs

they stay away because the rain won't come...


## *WATCHING THE WORLD GO BY LIKE A COUNTRY OF DOGS*

she's been staring at me
the whole time
with that look on her face
the girl
sitting in front of the fat  fuck
the ugly fuck with the stretch-marked love handles fighting for
supremacy with a gut too large for a hippo let alone a human being
maybe she wants to fuck me with her pierced nose
her pit stop lips
and her stocking clad legs
I wonder what it would be like for her
for fatso too
I wonder what it would be like for him
a virgin to anything but his hand and maybe a vacuum cleaner
she's clinging her purse now
maybe she wants to pay for it
maybe not
not here, not now
I must look like a treat
a testament to the pathetic chronicles of a [despot] poet the last of a
breed and the first as well like a fucked over automobile - the first in
a twenty car pile-up
I wonder how it would feel to sit in a truck stop in Sante-Fe
watching the world go by
like a country of dogs
and a fridge so cold all it does is warm the beer?
and that is where it lays

a life of words
a charity of hate
a blues song written to chill the soul of the most humble of
masterminds
a journey on the train
from nowhere to nowhere
where Dali doesn't paint anymore
where Burton is just the figment of his own two imaginations
and Bukowski still pushes the pencil from his lonely, drunk and
pessimistic grave
I look at her again
the woman that looks at me with those fuck me eyes
and she still stares
*later*
I whisper to her across the now packed sheep cart
*we stare today*
*later*
*maybe I will fuck you later...*


## MYSTERIOUS AND HOT

mysterious and hot
it leaves so many questions unanswered yet closes many others
new doors old doors/ doors/ that always seem to stay within and will
forever like a first love a first kiss a first death and the first taste of
hot and stinging liquor from a fine proofed bottle burning as it makes
its way down your throat to settle into your gut and merge with your
system creating the desire to sip again like some women do when
more never seems enough yet all that is sought is less

mysterious
and hot

no time like the present time when time is something that is short
like the end of the stick that always seems to reside in your hand
at the end of the day the end of the year and most likely the end
of your life when that end arrives today tomorrow next week or
however that's determined the way all determinations are made for
you by life law politics and women of past of present of future

questions
questions
questions
yes

mysterious
and hot
and as always
*of women...*

## LIKE A WOMAN WALKING TOWARDS YOU BUT BACKWARDS

nothing makes sense
in a world that spins the wrong way

......................................

like a woman walking towards you
but backwards

...................................

grasping realities and determining fantasies
never quite seemed so hard as it does through
nights of rain
songs of pain
and verses
written with a pen in contempt for what is sane

......................................

no more nights
no more days
where the breeze is cold but the company warm
no more smiles
no more thoughts
carried in synchronization
and voiced in unison
no more joy
no more insane
no more dreams of reality which are threaded with

the needles of a past better forgotten than
endured forever

...........................................

split in two
but not in balance
crying out names that no one wants to hear
shaken
stirred
shaken again
a martini at the merciless hands of a bartender not sure what to
tend

...........................................

and then it comes
your time to speak
the crowds - gathering
waiting to hear that wisdom you are so renown for
you stand at the podium of a life gone sour
the grey masses silenced in anticipation
and all that parts your parched lips are the words

I love her...


## IN THE BOTTOM OF A BOTTLE

I went to bed
and fucked her
but I felt nothing
so I stopped
got out of bed
to sit in the dark
and wonder
about life again
in the bottom of a bottle

## LAST WEEK

I saved an old woman/s life last week.
All of seventy she must have been.
Maybe I shouldn't have.
Maybe she didn't want it saved.
I wondered about it most of the day.
Whether being that old I would want someone saving mine.

Fuck old.

Right or wrong,
I saved an old woman/s life last week.


## FOR SALE

for sale
soul
damaged
cheap cheap cheap
possibly irreparable
willing to sell with dead liver black lungs broken heart and no real
desire to exist…


## REFUSE

skeletons raping skeletons
while new blood reads the morning papers
and out of reach
is just self-inflicted dissatisfaction
at milk gone sour
and light that refuses to penetrate the darkness any longer


## IRISH BREAKFAST AND THE BALLAD OF THE RAIN

I sit
the rain mocks the silence around me with its force against the tin
roof of the porch
it's like a beggar screaming obscenities in the middle of a wake,

silence pierced where only ever silence was expected
yet no longer is it competition to my pelting and thumping heart
instead
together
they play a symphony of truth to the way I feel
the taste of the Irish Breakfast is exquisite
as it slides warmly along my tainted throat,
a love that I have learnt,
a comfort that I share in honest secret,
and a meaning lost to all but a special few
or maybe none
the two mean more to me than expected
the tea
the rain
never the same
not ever again
like childhood memories that seem so distant I hope to never lose
this moment in time
where all that I have wronged
and all that I have given away and up
are mine for a few moments more
if only in heart and mind
and still it rains
in waves of heaviness
like spoiled and tangled emotions
twisted agonies
and the bittersweet taste of the blood that fills my mouth
by the words I write
and the heartaches I endure
and the loves that I pine for each and every moment of my now
disputable existence
I sip
I close my eyes
I listen heartedly
and I truly feel in this very moment
the ballad of the rain

## DIFFERENCE

readers who read who enjoy who love who comment who put
down and then forget like fish in a bowl but I can't forget like those
golden swimmers who live in the bubbles and think (pretend?) they
are happy or believe or strive going about their days as wise as
they can be through observation turned to word and to book back
to word again then discarded from time from history from sunlight
like being an Eskimo in the Sahara where difference is obvious but
choice is not I speak to you I beg to you that should I be that one
lying at the edge dying at the edge of an endless road that you take
care to step over me and let me go within the dream I have created
for myself

## BUTTERFLIES IN A SUMMER MONSOON

Gin
Like the poor man/s cocaine
Fucked over
It's all the very same
Sitting on a brick letterbox
Naked
In the wee hours
Of a morning
Too young
I should not have  been there
Yet I was
Floating
In the mists of a
One degree morning
Wondering why
The streetlights
Curled
And
Twisted
Around me
Instead of remaining
Stationary
Like they should be
Sitting on a brick letterbox

Naked
In the wee hours of a
One degree morning
Where the cold does not exist
Replaced by numb
Numb mind
Numb body
No one can
Help
Me
Now
Not that I feel visible
In the Darkness that festers within
Gin
It doesn't come quick enough
Leaves too soon
Like butterflies in a
Summer monsoon
When it seems
It's
All
You
Have


## AN OLD WHORE

people

the stain and the stench on your travel to death

a blatant rub in the face

I am the peasant you have created the peasant you want me to be
and the darkness you will always see or seek or not

you are a snake charmer programmed to charm the humanity that
is so well hidden within

don't fight me - you won't win - don't frighten me - you will pay -
don't love me - for you will eventually take that away

but

do fear me because what you want is bound and congealed is me is all I offer

and all I take your very thought and crush it and eat it and spit it out

before you get the chance
to
do
it
to
me

maybe I am that footpath that leads you to your destination the support for your muddy bloody size nines as they cover me with those who have suffered before

maybe not
maybe not
maybe not

kill me
kill me
kill me gently
when you brush off your pen and caress your pad, and once done scatter me to the homeless so that I too may live the cold in eternal salvation for heart, for soul

you are a destruction born of want
and
everything in between

hold me
hold me
hold me tightly
like you would hold yourself and put me to sleep
to slumber
to darkness
to grey

and one day

raise me again in a time when sun is norm and light is fervent (like
me to you and you to me) and death no longer says *I am your friend*
from the corner of a snide mouth and dry lips

then fuck me over once more

I am an old whore
too sore
to whore
any
any
any more

and

I am the statue that stands invisible beside your bed in eternity
but I am not angry anymore
I am just very
very
very sad...


## A RETURN JOURNEY

I know now where I'm going
the place I am being drawn toward
that familiar place
where dark is good and light is pain
where art no longer exists and sight is merely inconvenience
a hidden world
safe
where no one can find me and the birds don't sing to remind me of
all I desire
where women and men no longer exist and the stars are just
memories of times where love could be written and lived
no longer
soon
a place where politics is just a term for my own justifications of ill-
content
nothing more
than an existence void of colour

no love
no desire
no disappointment
no discontent
no lies
no hurt
no one
never
but safe
I know now
where I'm going because I've been there before
cold but warm
dark but light
there
where I must be safe
behind
the
wall...


## *A CLOCK TOO LOUD*

I look at the walls and remember what it's like to live
I look at the swirling mess in the ashtray and remember what it's
like to slowly kill myself
I look at the specs of dirt on the lived floor and wonder of the stories
that each hold sacredly hidden by age
I sit surrounded by my years of writing
years of useless words on useless and random paper
and wonder why I sit in the same place
the same way I did
1
10
50
100 years before
the same thoughts
the same confusion
the same love
the same pain
the same darkness mocking and cruel and mysterious and not

willing to budge like the footing of the right cemented firmly in the
foundations of history and the books of recorded truth
sometimes what seems like random can really be something so
[unconditionally]
structured
no figment of a Nostradamus but a defined and well thought
brushstroke made by a master
thought about for days
weeks
years
decades
centuries
never spoken about like memories of a dark and chilled prison of
conscious torture or the need to kill in an effort to save yourself
I look at the silence and emptiness around me and attempt at
reason
at solution
while always wondering just why here is where I must be living
sadness
and
madness
at each movement of the hand on a clock too loud...


## OF 20 OF 60

It doesn't matter / Whether you are / 20 / Or 60 / It all smells the
same / It all feels the same / Love / And torment / The gutters of
society / Life / Like screwed paper / Thrown in the waste basket /
And milk / Left to rot on the sill / Of an abandoned house / Like hope
/ Always there / Rarely given to / I wonder why I sit here / Tonight /
Writing discontent / A warm lamp / Reminding me of / Warmer times
/ Blue skies / No longer desired / Instead / Replaced by a winter /
Chill / And pouring rain / That seems / So much more / Palatable /
Than ever before / The mistakes of future / Weighing heavily / By
the mistakes / Of past / I wonder / About those shadows / Their
meaning / And purpose / As I wonder why / Heartache / Drew me to
stand / In the middle of that / Road / As my future / Drove rapidly /
Away from me / And my feet hurt / From the day / My mind from the
/ Passion / My soul through / Sadness / The red of tail lights / Never

seemed / So / Significant / In abandonment / In that very moment
/ Only to be / Complimented / By / Restless nights / Where sleep
is stolen / By conscious and unconscious / Fantasy / And links to
the forbidden / And a hatred / For time / For ropes and chains / Of
(perhaps?) breakable / Constraint / Where the slightest of / Space /
Of / Air / Between seems too much / To bare / At times / And though
the cycle / Has moved so far / Forward / And a future seems / So
much more / Possible / There still remains / The un-finished book
/ Of that 20 / Or 60 / Of difference / In the mind of one / And / In-
difference / To the other / Walking through puddles / To get your feet
wet / Is nothing / Without the rain / That creates in the beginning /
A pen in the hand of 20 / One in that of 60 / Yet again / They write /
The right / To be / And exist / And live / Without stepping / Ignorantly
/ Over the myths / That / Fight too hard / Too well / Sometimes /
Even though / Different / Is what is expected / And so / They / Dust
off the tome / That was shelved / So long ago / But never / Kept
too far / From reach / And / As the blown dust / Still / Lingers in the
damp air / Seeking / A place to rest / To settle / To decide / So it is /
That they float / Amidst this dust / This echo of time / Hoping / That
when finally / All is settled / And the room / Is calm / It is nestled
next to each other / With broken restraint / They share / The writing /
Of the next  Chapter / Of 20 / And of 60...


## BOSKANNA WAY

his name was Joe
he told me to meet him in a small street they call Boskanna Way

when I arrived he told me about his plans to take over the world
with his army of hookers
(Joe ran himself a brothel once on the south side of town - the real
dirty type - whores who'd do anything for a single dollar bill)

he had one of his hookers standing by his side
one he called ostascious
tall and skinny with jet black hair that looked like it had been cut with
a pair of child's scissors
she was one of those types

the type you see that are so ugly they border on being the most
beautiful in the world
Marxist eyes
blue tracks on skinny arms and black jeans torn in all the wrong
places
she held a book in her hand on guerrilla warfare and I could see a
switch blade sticking out from one of her tight front pockets
her lips were corpse blue and her eyes squinty like a crossed
Chinese girl in too bright sunlight
modern art with no room for elegance or tradition and the sound of
Lennon following her every step
her life just a pair of open legs and broken promises

and mine?

the same...


## PEOPLE

like cobras
ready to pounce at the slightest hint of movement before their
gleaming eyes

people

whose business is to know other people/s business
waiting to strike out when gossip comes their way

people

like cobras
striking out in fear of themselves
of being left behind or worse

lonely

people

just road kill

## CHASING

chasing rain love loneliness heartache pain women guns shoes
movies the jungle black vision no vision hurt hurt hurt confusion
tearing apart together apart nearly close so close

I want to say *you know I'm in love with her don't you?* but would she
ever listen? understand? forget? forgive?

....

(in the early hours of the morning) as my future lies restless before
me
*I think you've lost me* are the words that depart my lips

....

cold days colder nights I'm here again I hope you remember me

....

rocks no pumpkins and a desire to sink into the earth

....

lock your doors
drive safely
and watch out for mosquitos

....

and then I killed the sun before it killed me


## I WANT

I sit here in this place of caffeine
(feeling that these are places I no longer belong)
staring out the windows at people moving by with places to go and
things to do
trying my hardest
(to find inspiration to write)

saddened at the lack of success

I see a woman
with bright red hair and I want to fuck her because she reminds me
so much of what I have

I see another woman
all 'dolled' up and I want to fuck her because she reminds me of
what I could have had (and how glad I am I don't)

I see a man
in a suit and tie and I want to kill him for all the shit he and his suited
cronies have created in this world

a chronicle of destruction of society and of despair


## 40 YEARS

My room is just a space covered in clothes and smelling like drying
sex.
My mind's much the same.
40 years.
40 years spent conquering things that should never be conquered.
40 years of fuck up and avoidable pain,
of making love to fantasies and then killing them -
- sometimes slowly and at others with the flick of a hardened voice.
40 years.
40 fucking years and still,

IT ALL SEEMS SO FUCKING POINTLESS...

# DON'T GIVE UP

## *About the Author*

Among many other things Sean King claims to have studied at university in the fields of Art, Architecture, Literature and Journalism. This might well be so - there is no evidence to the contrary. Recently he was the owner/editor of a much-vaunted magazine for creative types called 'Finger' and from that endeavor alone one immediately gets a sense of what values drive Sean onward to greater glories. The author of over a thousand poems, thirty short stories and nine film scripts one wonders where he finds the time to finish writing his two in-progress novels. The owner of a dog, a motor bike and a swimming pool, Sean King is a one-man industry in ongoing re-development. His poetry book '*Empire of the Mind*' was first published in May 2009. A whizz on Guitar Hero and with a great eye for visual and visceral aesthetics, you can catch up with Sean (if you're fast enough) at www.seankingonline.com.